WRITTEN BY LAUREN FLAKE   ILLUSTRATED BY LAUREN FLAK

Where Did My Sweet Grandpa Go?

A Preschooler's Guide to Losing a Loved One

In memory of

ORVILLE RUSSELL BENTON

1922–2016

The author extends a special thank you to her husband, Travis,
for his support and encouragement throughout the publishing process.

loveofdixie

Published by
For the Love of Dixie, LLC
loveofdixie.com

Design by Monica Thomas for TLC Graphics, *www.TLCGraphics.com*

Illustrations by Lauren Flake and Dixie Benton Stucky

Graphics by various contributors. Cover: Grandpa and child by Lauren Flake; Interior: Pg 3 Fishing art
@ssstocker Depositphotos.com; Pg 5 Jellyfish by Dixie Benton Stucky; Pg 6 Leaves in wind ©ngaga35
Depositphotos.com; Pg 7 Trees by Lauren Flake; Pg 8 Birds ©gizele Depositphotos.com; Pg 9 Birds by Dixie
Benton Stucky; Pg 10 Paint brushes ©helehenogo Depositphotos.com; Pg 11 Canvas by Lauren Flake; Pg 12
Meadow © tawng Depositphotos.com; Pg 13 Mustangs by Dixie Benton Stucky; Pg 14 Love Music ©misima
Depositphotos.com; Pg 15 Child making music by Dixie Benton Stucky; Pg 17 Moon by Lauren Flake; Pg 19
Rainbow by Lauren Flake; Pg 20 Children at play ©hibrida13 Depositphotos.com; Pg 21 Butterfly by Dixie
Benton Stucky; Pg 23 Heart Puzzle by Lauren Flake; Back cover author photo ©Hilary Roberts Photography.

Where did my sweet
grandpa go?

Where is he?
I do not know.

Is he in the ocean blue,
Rolling in the waves
so true?

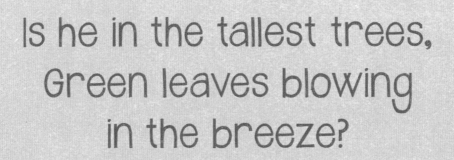

Is he in the tallest trees,
Green leaves blowing
in the breeze?

Is he in the sunny sky,
A handsome bird
flying high?

Is he in the artist's brush,
Colors across
canvas rush?

Is he on the open range,
Running free,
a wild mustang?

Is he in the songs we sing,
The sound of love and
joy we bring?

Is he in our dreams at night,
When we're tucked in bed
so tight?

Where did my sweet
grandpa go?

To be with God,
who loves us so.

He lives on in each new day,
In the way we live
and play.

Grandpa's in our hearts,
you see—
A special piece of
you and me.

For God so loved the world
that he gave his one and only Son,
that whoever believes in him
shall not perish but
have eternal life.

John 3:16 (NIV)

NOTE TO PARENTS

When my oldest daughter, who was two-and-a-half at the time, started asking questions about my mom, a year after she died, I wasn't quite sure where to begin.

She had been too young to understand at the funeral. She knew what Grandma Dixie looked like; she could point her out in photos. But she didn't understand where she was. I tried to explain that my mother wasn't here anymore, that she had died and was now in heaven.

When I asked if she knew Grandma Dixie, she replied confidently, "Yes." "What does she look like?" I said. I expected her to give a descriptor, like, "She has brown hair." Her response? "A bird. A pretty bird."

Then and there, the idea for this book's companion, *Where Did My Sweet Grandma Go?*, was born. My daughter continued to easily recognize my mother in framed photos displayed throughout our home, but she stood by her answer. Leaning on my clever little one for inspiration, I created a series of rhyming text and gentle nature scenes in hopes of answering her questions.

A few months later, we lost my stepmom and then my husband's grandfather, and I realized that our story might help other children beyond my own daughters. It seemed only fitting to incorporate pieces of my mother's artwork with my own to illustrate this tender lesson about enduring legacy.

These days, I talk to my three- and five-year-old daughters about spiritual concepts like heaven, God's grace, and eternal life more easily, but it can be very difficult to help little ones deal with death and loss while we are in the midst of our own grief. Losing my maternal grandfather immediately following *Sweet Grandma*'s release inspired me to create this book.

Because most preschool-age children cannot fully grasp the permanence of death, I believe our most important task, as parents of grieving preschoolers, is to model what healthy grief looks like. We should always reassure them that negative emotions, like anger and sadness, are a necessary and normal part of healing. But we should also reassure them that, because our loved ones are an eternal piece of God's creation, they can never really be lost.

My prayer is that this book will give your family a starting point for heartfelt conversations about life, death, loss, and, most importantly, love.

Lauren

PARENTS' GUIDE

QUESTIONS

- What do you know or remember about [name of loved one]? Can you think of something that they gave or taught us? How do you feel when you see or think about those things?

- Why do you think it's good to talk about [name of loved one]? How we can remember them each day? What can we do with what they gave or taught us?

  You can alternatively ask your child to draw or paint pictures, using these questions as prompts.

ACTIVITIES

- Donate to or volunteer at a ministry or charity that was near and dear to your loved one's heart.

- Make a pillow, quilt, or stuffed animal out of your loved one's favorite clothing.

- Spend a special day, such as your loved one's birthday, at one of their favorite places, listening to their favorite music, or eating some of their favorite foods.

- Create a memorial garden in your backyard with your loved one's favorite plants, statues of their favorite animals, a special bench, a bird feeder, or stepping stones.

- Assemble a shadow box, photo book, or collage to display memories of your loved one.

- Attend a class, workshop, or museum where you can learn about your loved one's favorite skill or hobby.

- Write a letter to your loved one, expressing your love and gratitude for them.

~ BIBLE PASSAGES ~

- Read Matthew 5:1-10 and Ecclesiastes 3:1-8. Did you know that Jesus feels our hurt and comforts us when we are missing [name of loved one]? God already knows when each of his children will be born and when they will die. We are all a part of God's great, big plan for his creation, and he invites each of us to spend eternity with him in heaven.

~ RESOURCES ~

- Watch Disney/Pixar's *Inside Out* (2015). Riley learns that grief is a normal, healthy response when we lose something that we love. We can only experience Joy if we are willing to acknowledge Sadness.

- Watch *Charlotte's Web* (2006) and Disney's *The Lion King* (1994). Alternatively, read *Charlotte's Web* by E.B. White. When Charlotte and Mufasa die, they live on in their children. Our loved ones are never really gone because they will always be a part of us.

- Read *God Gave Us Heaven* by Lisa T. Bergren and *The Jesus Storybook Bible* by Sally Lloyd-Jones. God offers us a place in heaven through his infinite grace and love.

Made in the USA
Las Vegas, NV
13 December 2022

62137413R00019